Contents   Page

Contents   Page

Contents	Page

Before you access AutoCAD

Before accessing AutoCAD

1.After opening the autocad program, press New
as shown in Figure a.

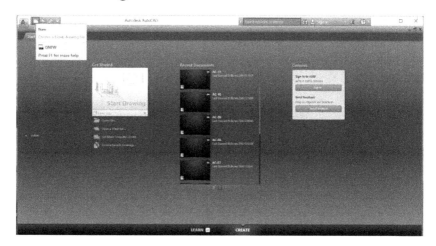

Figure A

2.Then click to select acadiso as shown in Figure
b.

3.After entering the autocad drawing window, press Ctrl + Shift + right-click and select Osnap Setting as shown in Figure c.

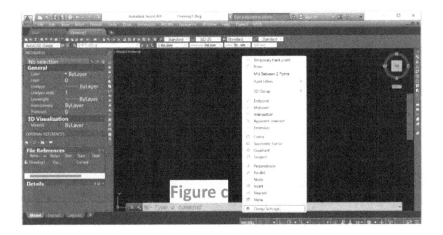

4.Then select all and press OK to turn on all snap modes for easy writing.

Chapter 1

Basic commands used in drawings

Chapter 1 Basic commands used in drawings

1.1Line Command

- To start, enter the Line command by Type according to Figure 1.1a and press Enter.

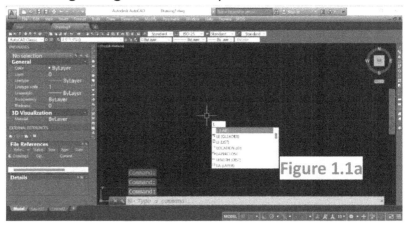

Figure 1.1a

- Then drag the line by left-clicking from where we want to start drawing 1 time and then drag the mouse or drag the line to the desired direction. While stroke, F8 may be pressed to force the drawn line to be in the X or Y axis. When you get the desired distance, left-click 1 time and press Esc or Enter or Space Bar to exit the command , or you can enter the desired distance during stroke, such as the distance of 800 units as shown in Figure 1.1b, then press

Enter to confirm and press exit from the Esc
command .

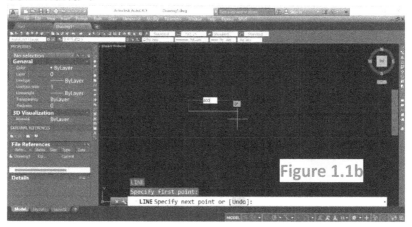

Figure 1.1b

1.2 Zoom in and out and PAN using mouse

- Start after we get a straight line, try to arrange
the page view as shown in Figure 1.2a by using
the mouse, starting by holding down the mouse
roller and dragging the mouse to change the
perspective (there may be some release to
divide the stroke of dragging several times. for
ease of changing the view.) During this time,
zooming in and out may be Use the mouse
roller to roll up and down (up equals zoom in,
down equals zoom out) to make changing views
more convenient.

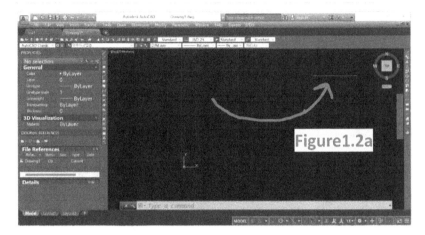

Figure1.2a

1.3 Polyline command

- Start Type pl as the command and press enter as shown in Figure 1.3a is the same command as Line, but while drawing a line, it is possible to use commands other than Line such as arc as a command to   drag a curve after the line we drew earlier without having to press out of the command first, as shown in the picture. 1.3b is to enter the arc continuation command (type arc and press enter) and when we want to close the line loop that we draw, press c and press enter, it will close the loop. The line we draw (the command that hangs in the Command before closing the last loop should be a line command) as shown in Figure 1.3c and 1.3d will notice that the line we drag Polyline is the same object when left-clicking to line 1time as shown in Figure 1.3d

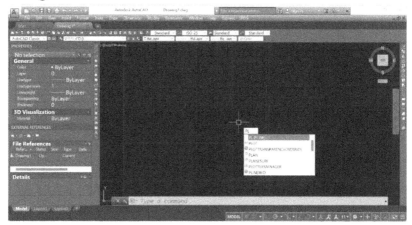

Figure1.3a

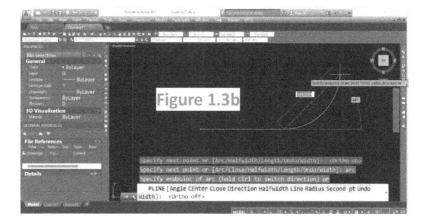

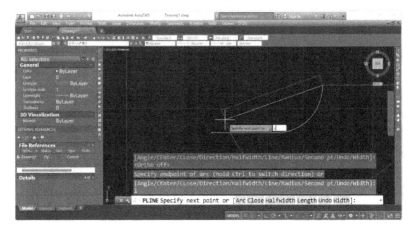

Figure 1.3c

Before closing the loop, it should first be changed to a line command. After using the arc command

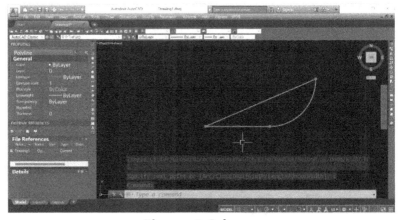

Figure 1.3d

1.4 MOVE COMMAND

-Start by selecting the object we want to move by clicking as shown in Figure 1.4a.

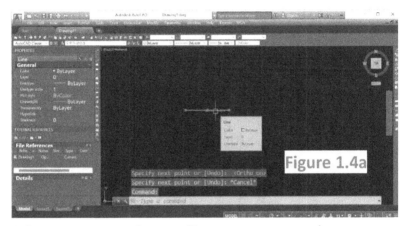

-Then type m and press Enter to execute the move command as shown in Figure 1.4b.

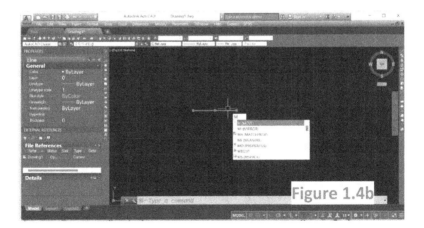

-Figure 1.4c selects the end of the line on the left by clicking to hit the green square Snap dot that appears. At the left end of the straight line when the mouse is placed. (We can close the Snap point by pressing F3 for easy drawing.)

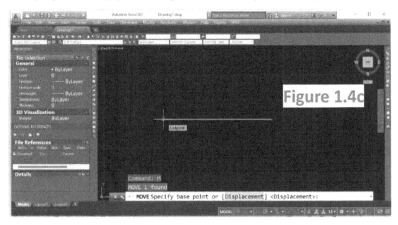

Figure 1.4c

-Then use the mouse to drag it to move the object to the desired position. In the meantime, press F8 to make the object move in the X or Y axis, and may use typing to indicate the distance of movement instead of using the mouse to click confirm. Move the object by dragging the mouse to the direction you want to move and type the distance to move how many units in Figure 1.4d 500 units and press Enter.

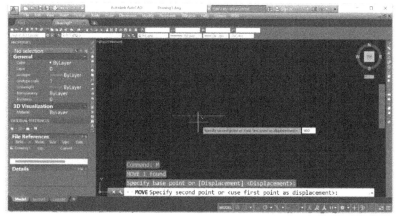

Figure 1.4d

1.5 Fillet command

- Start to create a straight line in the shape of an L as shown in Figure 1.5a, you can use the command Polyline or line.

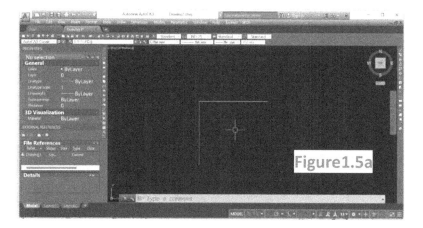

Figure 1.5a

-Then call the Fillet command by typing F as shown in Figure 1.5b and press Enter.

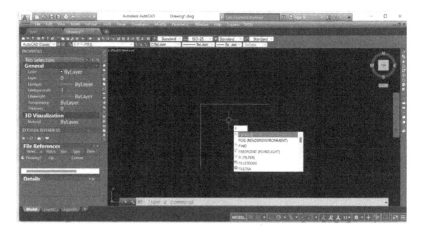

Figure 1.5b

-Then type R and Enter to enter the curve radius that we will Fillet as shown in Figure 1.5c, enter 200 units, and press Enter again.

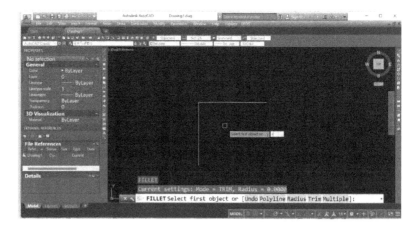

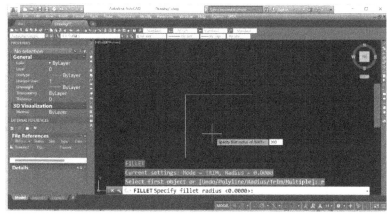

Figure 1.5c

-Then the cursor mouse will be rectangular,
press or click on the 2 straight lines that we
want Fillet to finish the Fillet command as
shown in the Figure 1.5d pics

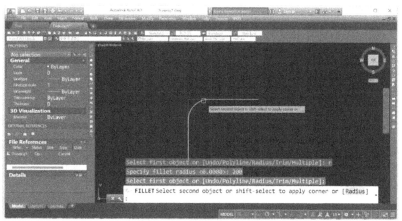

Figure 1.5d

1.6 Offset command

- We will offset the line out of the created straight line by initiating a command call. Type O and press Enter as shown in Figure 1.6a.

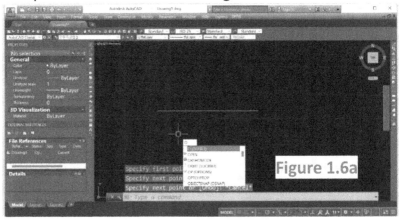

Figure 1.6a

-Then enter the Offset radius that we want by typing r and press ENTER and enter the value as shown in Figure 1.6b, enter the value to 200 units and press ENTER again.

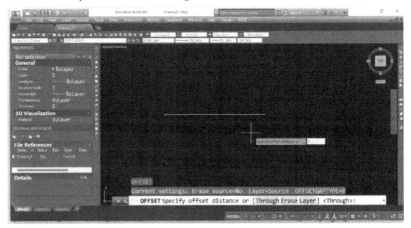

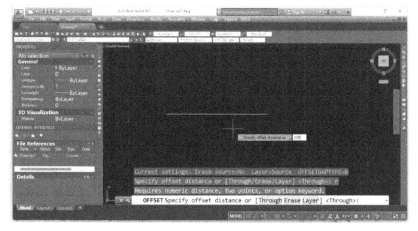

Figure 1.6b

-Then left-click on the line where we are going
to make it. Offset, sir. Click 1 time and drag the
mouse in the desired direction. Offset, as shown
in Figure 1.6C, will drag upwards without telling
the distance anymore. Click anywhere to finish.
Offset command, sir. Left click 1 time will offset
the line from the original line 200 units.

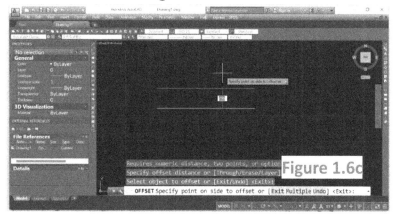

Figure 1.6c

1.7 COPY COMMAND

-START TO SELECT THE OBJECT THAT WE WANT TO COPY. By clicking as shown in Figure 1.7a in the figure, you will click the straight line created earlier.

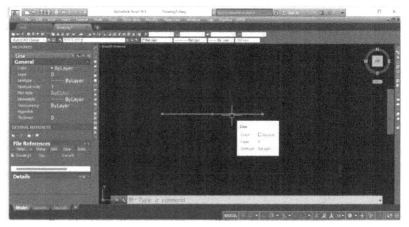

Figure1.7a

-Then type co and press Enter to execute the COPY command as shown in Figure 1.7b.

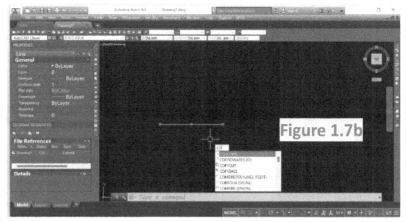

-As shown in Figure 1.7c, select the end of the straight line on the left by clicking to hit the green square Snap dot that appears. At the left end of the straight line when the mouse is placed. (We can close the Snap point by pressing F3 for easy drawing.)

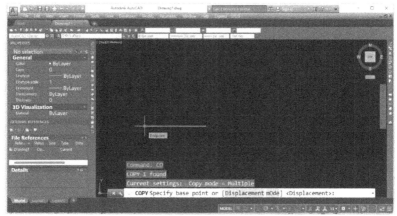

Figure 1.7c

-THEN USE THE MOUSE TO DRAG TO COPY THE OBJECT TO THE DESIRED LOCATION. In the meantime, press F8 to make the object move in the X or Y axis, and may use typing to indicate the distance of movement instead of using the mouse to click to confirm. COPY the object by dragging the mouse to the direction you want to copy and type the distance to copy how many units in Figure 1.7d 500 units and press Enter.

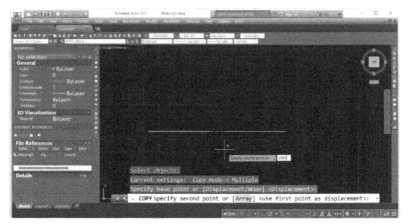

Figure 1.7d

1.8Trim Command

-To begin with, we will create a problem by creating intersecting lines into shapes. The cross is shown in Figure 1.8a using the Line command.

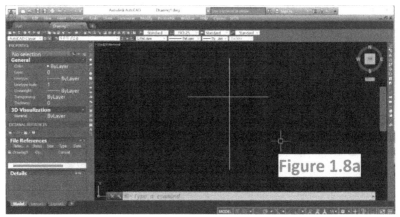

- Then we will cut out the line in the part we want to use, using the Trim command, type tr and press Enter, then click on the line that the reference used to cut excess from the reference line that we have selected.

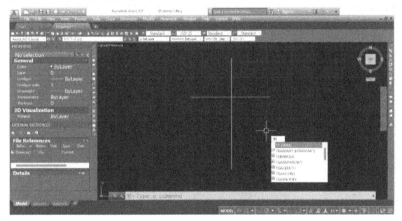

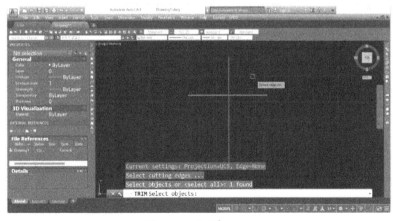

Figure 1.8b

-Then let us take the cursor mouse and place it where we want to cut the excess from the reference line that we have selected. As shown in Figure 1.8c, select the vertical line above that goes beyond the reference line, then click 1 time will cross the line.

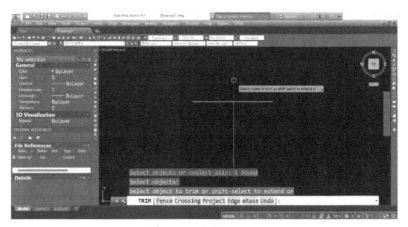

Figure 1.8c

1.9 Extent Command

-Start to create a large T-shaped line as shown in Figure 1.9a, but do not stick together.

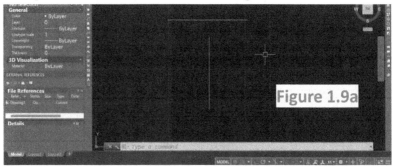

Figure 1.9a

-Then run the command. Type ex and press
Enter and select the reference line we want as
shown in Figure 1.9b, select the horizontal line
and press Enter again.

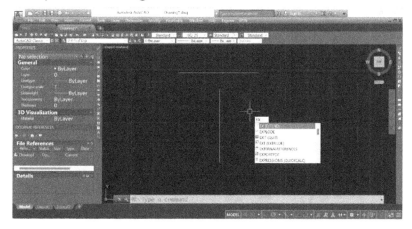

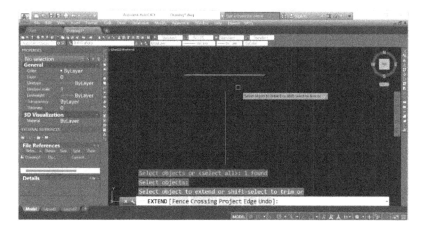

Figure 1.9b

-Then place the cursor mouse on the line we want to extent to stretch to hit the reference line we have selected as shown in Figure 1.9c and click 1 time to finish the command.

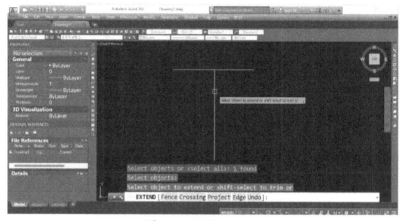

Figure 1.9c

1.10 Scale command

- Start us to create the piece we want. Scale as shown in Figure 1.10a may use Line or Poly Line command to create.

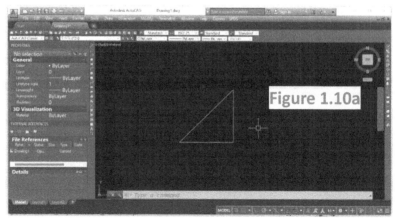

-Then run the command by typing sc and press Enter and click on the piece we want to scale, shrink or expand as shown in Figure 1.10b.
Press Enter.

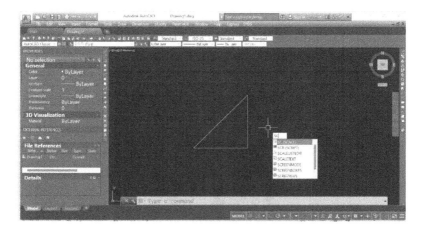

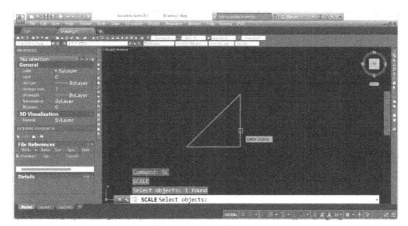

Figure 1.10b

-Then click on the reference point to shrink or enlarge the object (anywhere) as shown in Figure 1.10c, click on the lower left corner and enter the Scale value we want, for example, in the picture 1.10c, enter the number 3, meaning that the object size after Scale will be 3 times larger than the original , or if you enter the number 0.5,   it will be smaller than the original. Half.

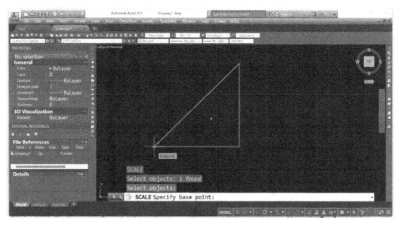

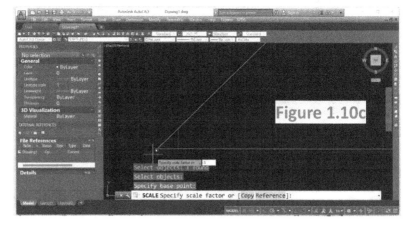

Figure 1.10c

-When you are finished entering press Enter will finish the command. As shown in the picture 1.10d, the object is 3 times larger than before.

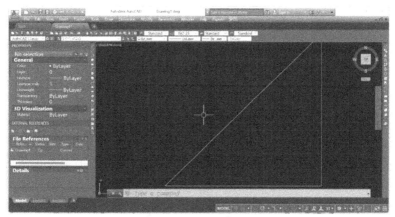

Figure 1.10d

-We may use the Scale reference command to scale the object to the same size as the reference object. To begin with, we will give an example by creating two identical pieces with different sizes, as shown in Figure 1.10F.

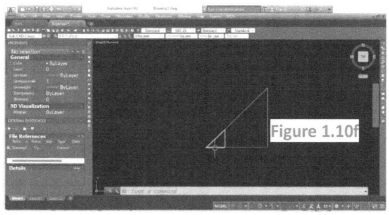

-Then we will give an example by Enlarge the image (small image) evenly with the larger image by Type the sc command and press Enter as shown in the 1.10g image. Click on the small object and press Enter and click the reference point of the object that we want to scale.

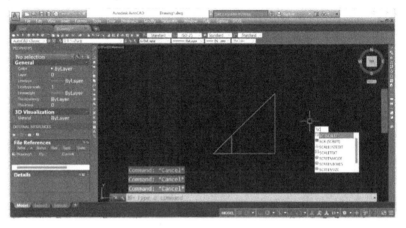

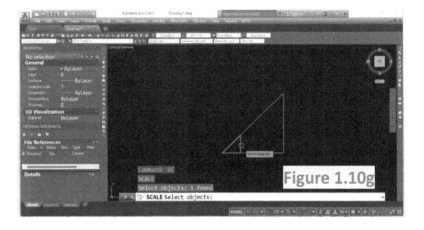

Figure 1.10g

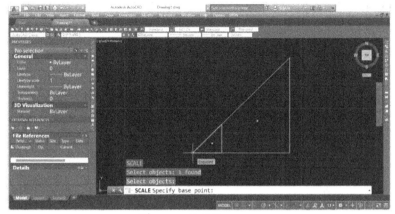

Figure 1.10g

-Next, type r and press Enter as shown in the
Figure 1.10h

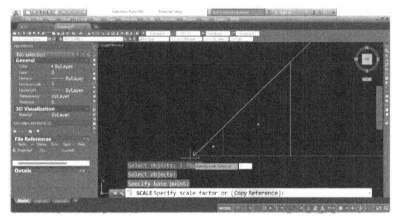

Figure 1.10h

-afterwards Click on the left end of the object as it is, then click on the top of the triangle as shown in Figure 1.10I.

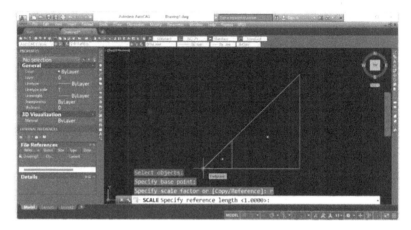

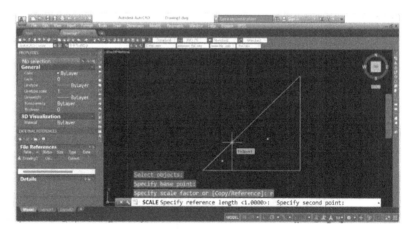

Figure 1.10I

-Then drag the mouse to collide with the triangular top of the big picture, and it's over. command now The small object is then the size of the large image and is stacked as shown in Figure 1.10J.

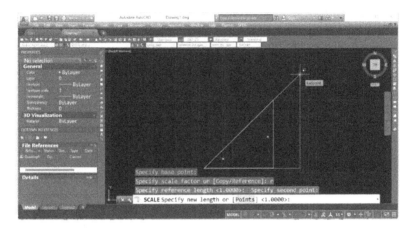

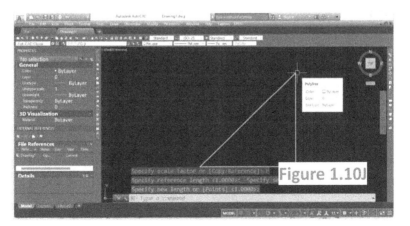

Figure 1.10J

1.11 Rotate Command

- Let us start to create the workpiece in order to rotate first as shown in Figure 1.11a.

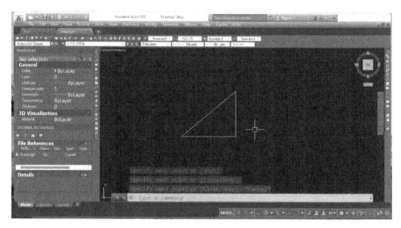

Figure 1.11a

-Then call the Rotate command by typing ro and pressing enter as shown in Figure 1.11b.

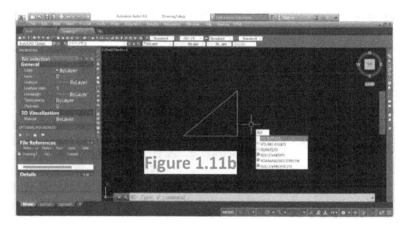

-Then click on the object we want to rotate.
When you click on Finish, press Enter as shown
in Figure 1.11c.

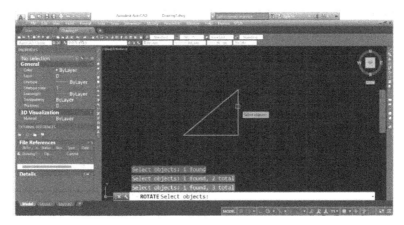

Figure 1.11c

-Click the reference position to Rotate as shown
in Figure 1.11d. triangle

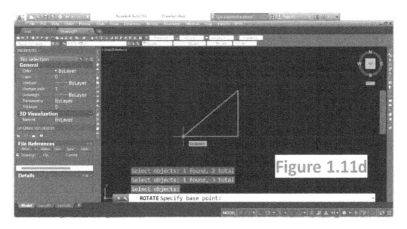

-Use the mouse to drag to rotate the object to the desired position. In the meantime, press F8 to make the object rotate in the X or Y axis, or you may use the rotation degree input as shown in the picture 1.11e, enter 90 is rotate counter-needle to 90 degrees. Enter it and press Enter to end the command.

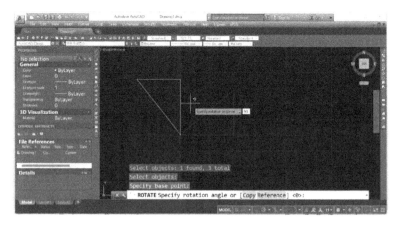

Figure 1.11e

1.12 Mirror command

- Let us create a piece that will mirror first, as shown in Figure 1.12a.

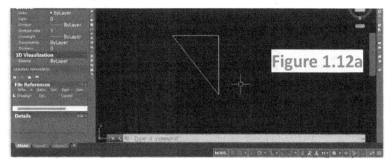

-Then run the Mirror command, type mi and press enter as shown in picture 1.12b.

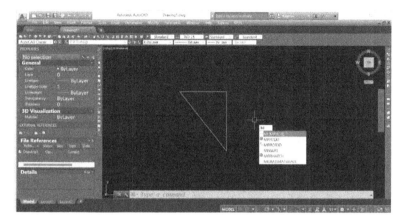

Figure 1.12b

-Click on the object we want to mirror or mirror when finished, press Enter as shown in Figure 1.12c.

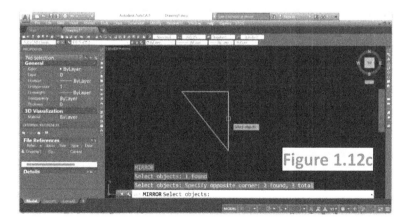

-Click to create a mirror to create a mirror object anywhere as shown in Figure 1.12d to create a vertical mirror by clicking on the empty space 1 time and dragging the mouse down as shown in the picture. At any distance, click 1 more time.

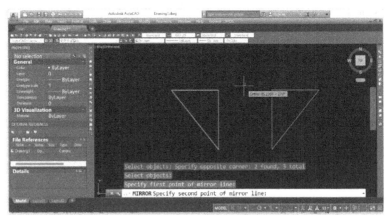

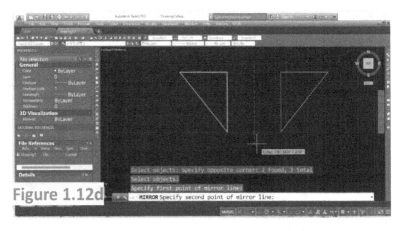

Figure 1.12d

-The program then asks if we will remove the old object as well after reflecting the object. Type N is not deleted. Type Y is to be deleted, as shown in the Figure 1.12e . N and press enter (use the mouse to click No as shown in the picture) will end the command.

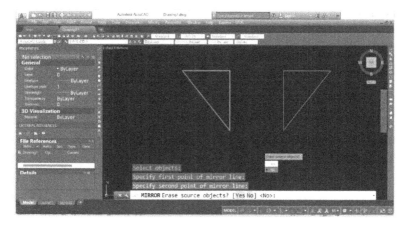

Figure 1.12e

1.13 Create Square command

-Start Call the command by typing rec as shown in Figure 1.13a.

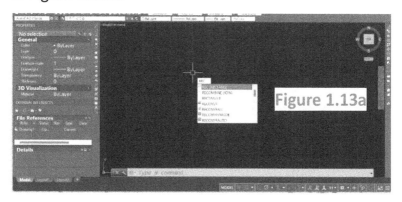

-Click the reference point to draw in any empty space with 1 Time as shown in Figure 1.13b.

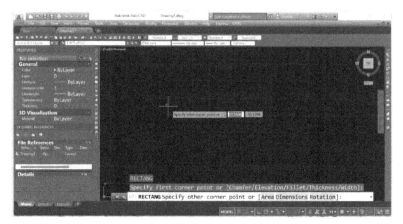

Figure 1.13b

-After clicking the waypoint in the drawing, Use the mouse to drag to draw the square as we want when you get and click 1 more time to finish the command as shown in the picture 1.13c.

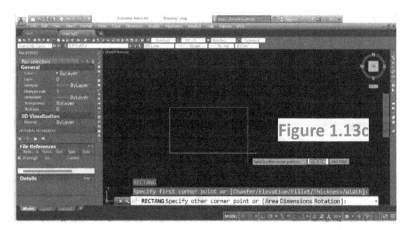

-Or after clicking the reference point in the drawing, you may use the method to tell the size before ordering the drawing by typing di and press Enter.

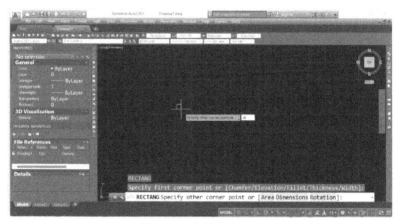

Figure 1.13d

-Enter the size of the rectangle we want by typing length first, press Enter and then Width and press Enter again as shown in Figure 1.13e.

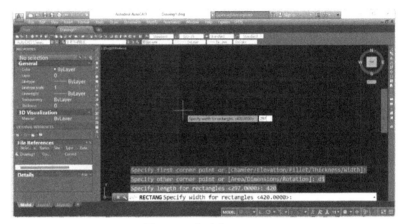

Figure 1.13e

-Then click anywhere 1 time to finish the command, as shown in Figure 1.13f.

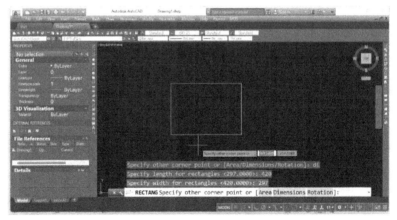

Figure 1.13f

1.14 Circle Creation Command

- Start calling the command by typing c and press Enter as shown in Figure 1.14a.

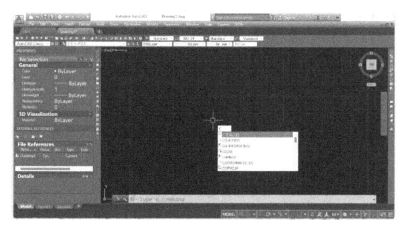

Figure 1.14a

-Then click on the reference point where we want to start drawing. Click 1 time as shown in Figure 1.14b.

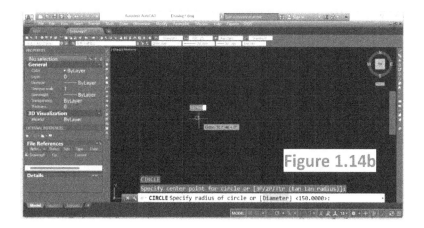

-After clicking on the waypoint in the drawing, then drag the mouse to draw the circle. When you get the desired distance and click 1 more time to finish the command as shown in Figure 1.14c.

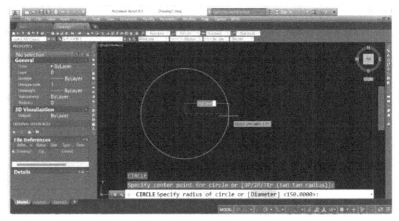

Figure 1.14c

-After clicking on a reference point in a drawing, sizing may be used before ordering the drawing. Drag the mouse for a while, then type radial circle in the picture 1.14d, type 150 units, and press Enter to finish the command.

1.15 Dimension command

-Let us first create a piece that will be sized according to Figure 1.15a as the workpiece. Squares and circles and triangles

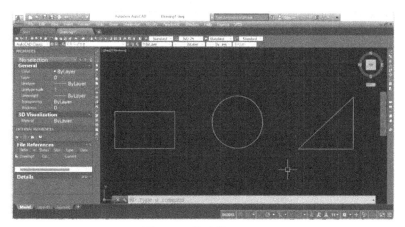

Figure 1.15a

-Then run the command by Type di and press Enter as shown in Figure 1.15b.

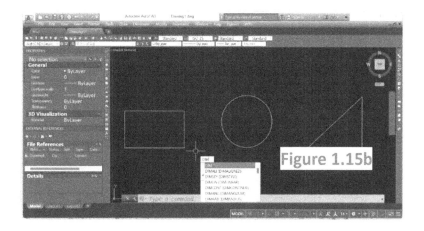

Figure 1.15b

-Click to measure the size of the object as we want by clicking Go to Start and drag the mouse and click Go to the end or end of the target we want. Now I know the size and 1 more time, I will notice that if it is a circle, put the mouse cursor on the picture, it will tell the diameter, so the arrow indicating the size will change according to the workpiece as shown in the picture 1.15c.

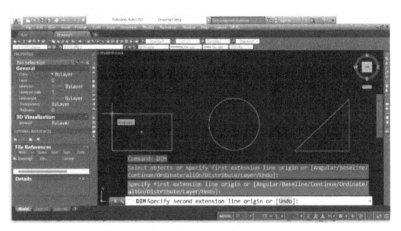

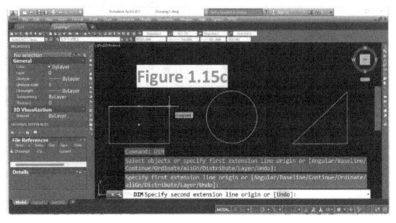

Figure 1.15c

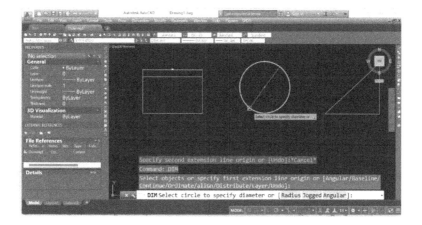

Figure 1.15c

-To measure the hypotenuse, a sizing command may be used based on Figure 1.15d.

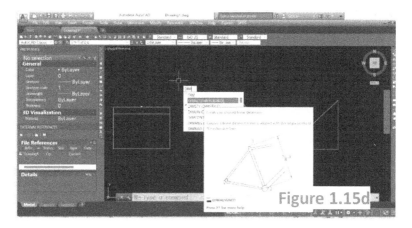

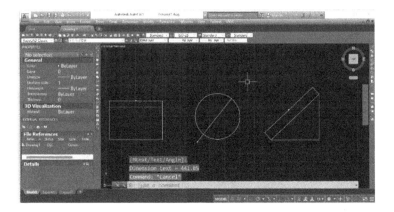

Figure 1.15d

- You can adjust the size of the arrows or text by going to Properties, clicking on the dimension time then pressing Mo, and then pressing ENTER.

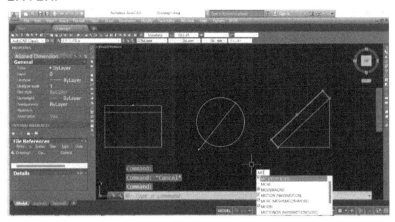

Figure 1.15e

-You will see the properties page of the size
guide as shown in Figure 1.15F, you can adjust
the value according to various categories such
as Line & Arrow, arrow size and type of arrow, or
Text text size.

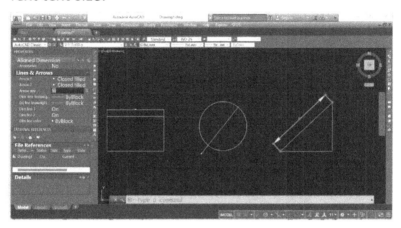

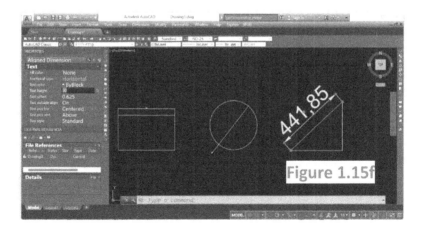

Figure 1.15f

-We can type in the numbers ourselves by
Double click on the text 1 time and type as
shown in the 1.15g image.

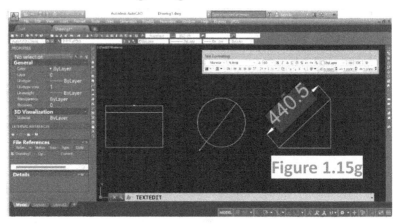

-To print the diameter symbol, type %%C .

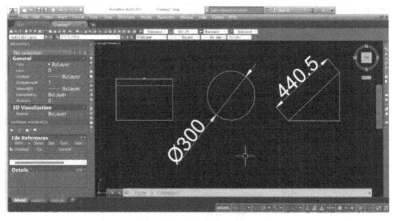

Figure 1.15g

1.16 Create Block and Extract Block commands

-Start us to create the piece as shown in Figure 1.16a using REC and LINE commands.

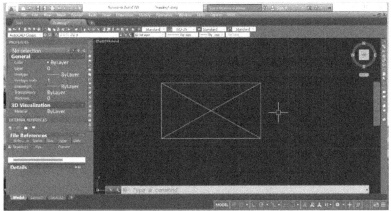

Figure 1.16a

-Then select all the objects and type b and press Enter as shown in Figure 1.16b.

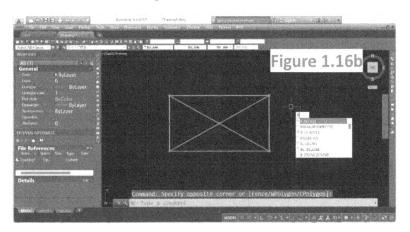

-Type in the name Block as shown in Figure 1.16c, name the block B1 . Press OK to finish the command.

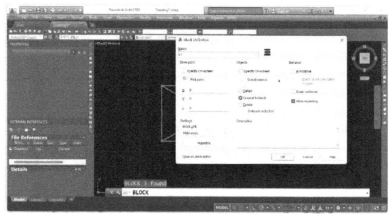

Figure 1.16c

-The object is now the same piece and we can edit the block or object by double-clicking it. Click on Object, then display the window as shown in Figure 1.16d and press OK .

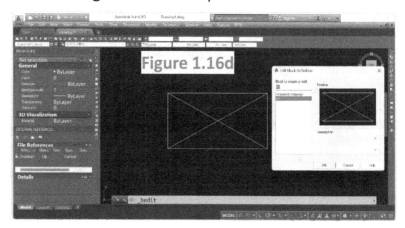

-We can customize Block B1, such as removing lines and cutting lines as in Figure 1.16e.

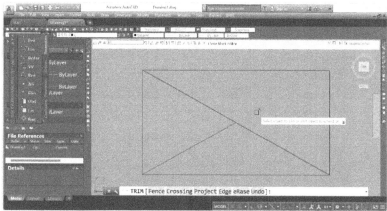

Figure 1.16e

-Once the editing is done, make a statement. Right click on an empty area, select Close Block Editor as shown in the 1.16f.

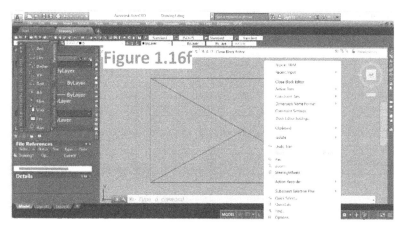

-Then press SAVE CHANGE to finish editing as shown in picture 1.16g.

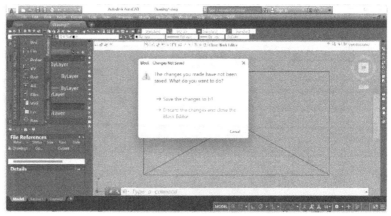

Figure 1.16g

-We can crack the block that we created by clicking on the block and then selecting it. Type x and press Enter as shown in the picture 1.16h.

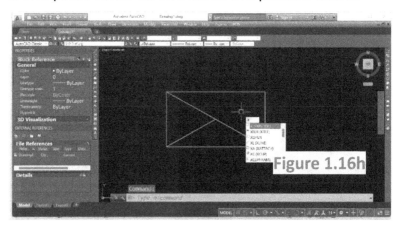

Figure 1.16h

1.17HATCH command

-Start creating polyline as shown in the picture or you can use the REC command as shown in Figure 1.17a.

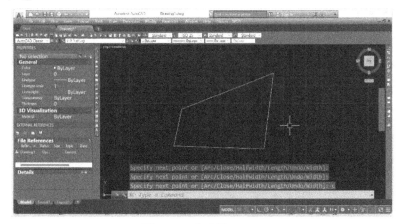

Figure 1.17a

-afterwards Call the command, type h and press ENTER as shown in Figure 1.17b.

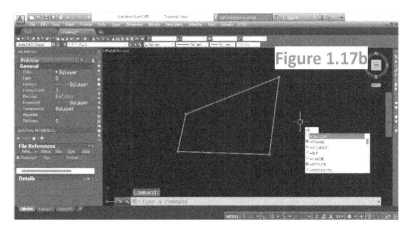

-The window will show as shown in Figure 1.17c
and click on the type of HATCH at swatch

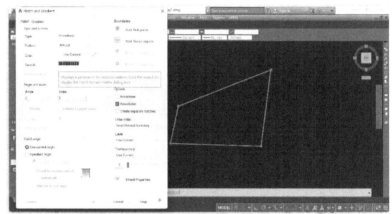

Figure 1.17c

-As shown in the 1.17d picture, most select ISO
and press OK.

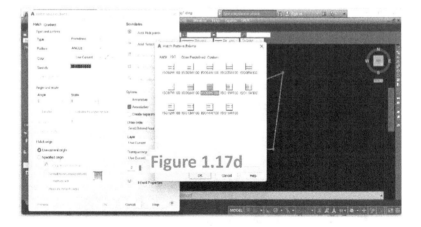

Figure 1.17d

-Then click to select Add Select Objects as
shown in Figure 1.17e.

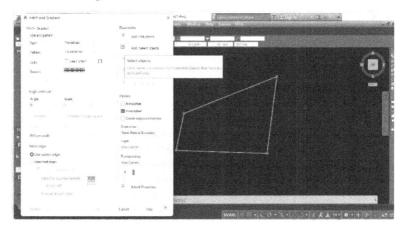

Figure 1.17e

-Then click on the HATCH boundary frame,
which is the polyline that we created itself as
shown in picture 1.17f, press Enter and then
press OK.

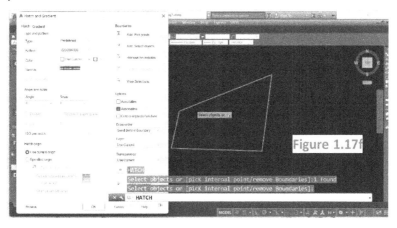

-We will have the HATCH line, according to the scope we choose. Click on HATCH 1 time and look at   Properties at Scale according to the 1.17g Surface . As in the picture, it is entered 10.

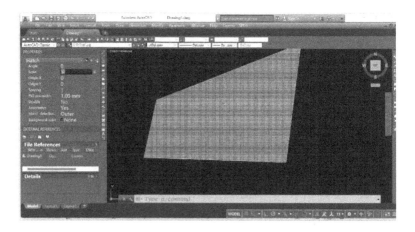

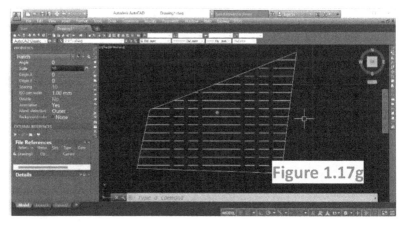

Figure 1.17g

1.18 Array Command

- To start, we make an object to be array as shown in the picture. 1.18a pics any size pics

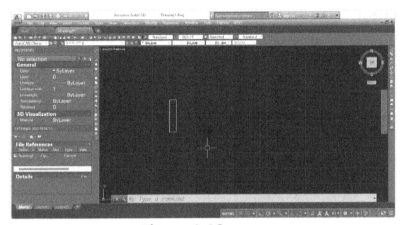

Figure 1.18a

-Then click on the object, type the ar command and press Enter, as shown in Figure 1.18b.

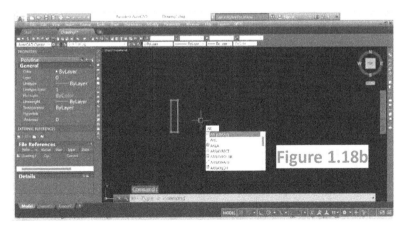

-We can choose the format of the array as shown in Figure 1.18c. Select rectangular is square (PATH is a straight line or along the line we choose, and Polar is circle)

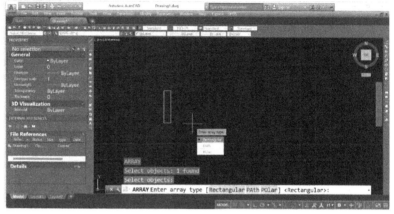

Figure 1.18c

-We can adjust the array by Click on the arrow as shown in the picture 1.18d and drag the mouse, stretch it and click 1 more time to finish the command and can enter the value to adjust the number of rows or digits by Change Row /Columns /Spacing according to the command below.

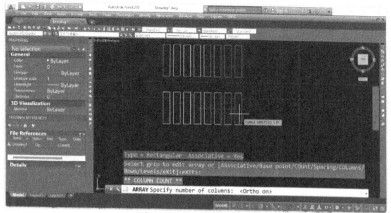

Figure 1.18d

1.19 TEXT command

- Start enter commands by Type text and press Enter as shown in Figure 1.19a.

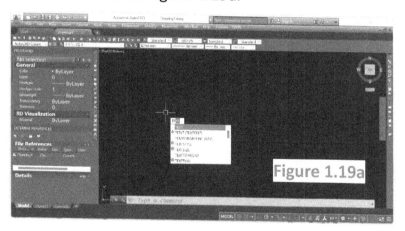

Figure 1.19a

-Then click to select the reference point to type
the text 1 time and drag the mouse. Print
Orientation As shown in Figure 1.19b, drag to
the right. Horizontal

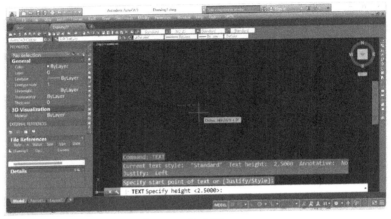

Figure 1.19b

-Drag it as far as you want because it just tells
you the orientation of the print. Double click
until Generate printing curser as shown in
Figure 1.19c.

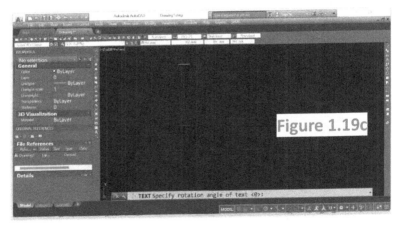

-Then type anything you want. Finished printing. Press double click exit and press Esc exit from the command to finish the command as shown in the picture 1.19d and as before, we can resize. If the Properties window does not appear, click on Text and type mo and press Enter.

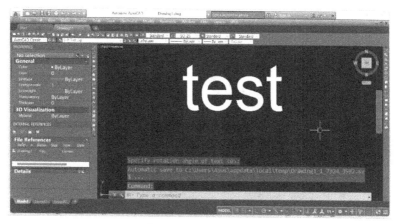

Figure 1.19d

1.20 Arrow commands

- Start the command by typing le and press ENTER as shown in Figure 1.20a.

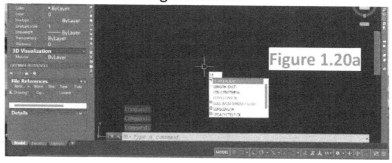

-Then start drawing the arrow by clicking on the point we want to point to 1 time and dragging the mouse to our narration. During this time, the arrow tail can click to change direction 2 times, during drag may press F8 to make the arrow tail line in the X or Y axis as shown in Figure 1.20b. Press ESC out of command.

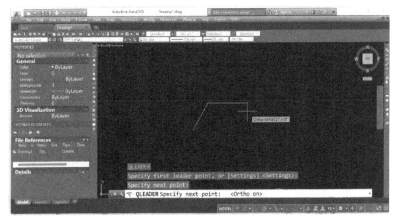

Figure 1.20b

-We can adjust the size or arrow type by going to Properties as shown in Figure 1.20c, resizing 150.

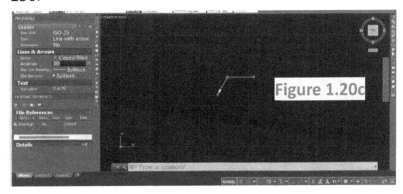

1.21 Summary of the various tricks in drawing

-Snap can be turned off by pressing F3.

-We can block in line or axial drag guide. X or Y by pressing F8.

-We can remove the object we have selected by holding down Shift and clicking on the object we want to remove from the selection.

-You can repeat the command by pressing the Space bar, reremembering the last command without having to type the command name repeatedly.

-In selecting an object, if we click 1 time and drag the mouse to the right, a blue cover area will be formed. This cover area must cover all the objects we have selected to be selected. As shown in Figure 1.21a.

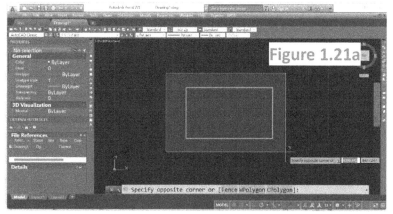

Figure 1.21a

-To select an object, if we click 1 time and drag the mouse to the left, a green cover will be formed.This cover area simply touches or touches the selected object to select all objects, as shown in Figure 1.21b.

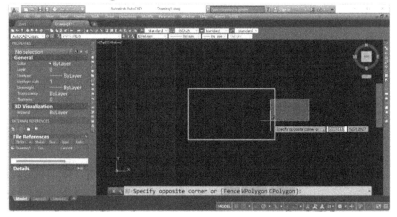

Figure 1.21b

-To exit the command we can press Esc Enter or Space bar.

-We can stretch the object without using the Extent command by clicking on the blue dot position as shown in Figure 1.21c and dragging the mouse.

Chapter 2

Manage Page Before Printing

Chapter 2 Manage Page Before Printing

2.1 Printing Page Layout Model Page Scale

-Start us to create an A3 page frame as shown
in the picture, which we will write in the mm
system, the method is to think that the unit we
write in mm is to create a long page frame 420
units long and 297 units wide as shown in
Figure 2.1a.There may be offset edge decoration
with title head as shown in the picture.

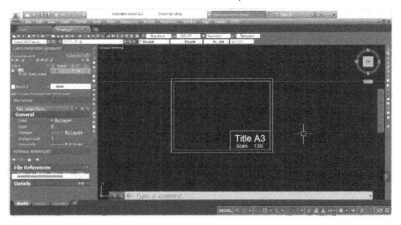

Figure 2.1a

- Then we will write a scale of 1:50 for us to expand. The page frame goes 50 times by using the sc command.

- In the paper frame we created to create the piece. This is a straight pipe size 20 inches long 8m (8000 units) as shown in Figure 2.1b. The letter size in the form is calculated by taking 1.8 x 50 = 90mm.

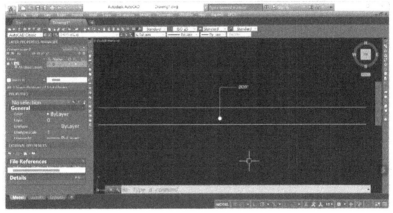

Figure 2.1b

-Then press Print, press Ctrl+P, set as shown in the picture, and press Window as shown in the picture 2.1c.

Figure 2.1c

-This is the paper   frame that we created by pressing the left click on the bottom left corner of the paper 1 time and press the top right corner of the paper frame 1 time as   shown in picture 2.1d.

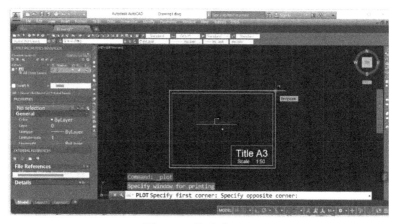

Figure 2.1d

-Then adjust the print size to 1mm : 50 units as shown in the picture and press Center Plot as shown in Figure 2.1e.

-Then press Preview to see that as shown in the picture 2.1f will get the picture OK and press Print to PDF order or you can order it out at all.

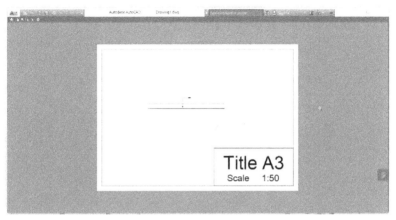

Figure 2.1f

2.2 Print Page Layout

- Start us to create an A3 paper frame, page model, before the same as before. mm yep as pictured 2.2a

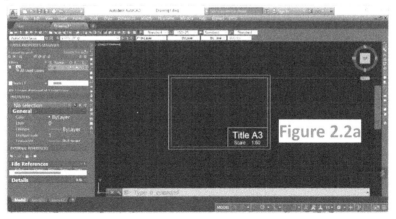

-Then make an A3 paper frame to be blocked.
Name it A3.

-Then you can see that the reference point
Block is located at the X,Y axis point or point 0,0
as shown in Figure 2.2b.

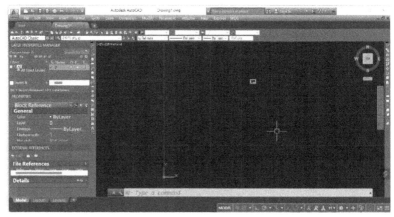

Figure 2.2b

-If the reference point is not on the workpiece,
go in and fix it. Block pics and catch The page
frame in the lower left corner is moved to
point 0,0 as shown in Figure 2.2c by taking
advantage of the Snap point at the end of the
straight line that exits the point 0,0 that we
created earlier. Type 0,0 and press Enter, we

will get a straight line out of point 0,0 and then left-click anywhere and press Esc   out.)

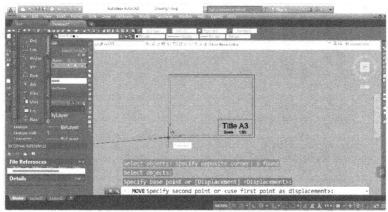

Figure 2.2c

-Then remove the straight line and exit the edit. Block by right-clicking and pressing Close Block Editor. The reference point block is now adjacent to the paper frame at point 0,0 as shown in Figure 2.2d.

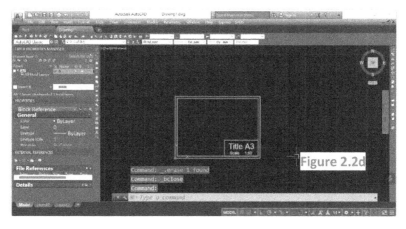

Figure 2.2d

-Go to the Layout page, press insert block A3 as shown in picture 2.2e.

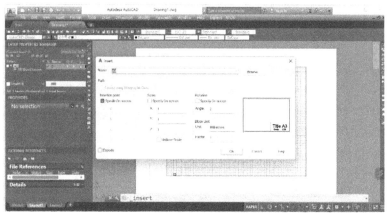

Figure 2.2e

-Then type 0,0 as shown in Figure 2.2f and press Enter, it will place the block at point 0,0 based on the reference point. Block, sir.

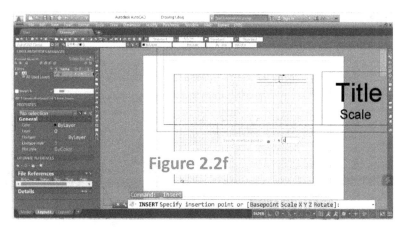

Figure 2.2f

-Then hold the frame to the inner frame of the paper. A3 as Figure 2.2g

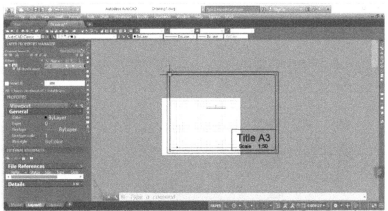

Figure 2.2g

-Then double-click on the framework and then click on it. Slide Pan to find our workpiece, that is a 20-inch pipe 8m long , then drag the cursor mouse outside the page frame and double click it out as shown in the picture 2.2h.

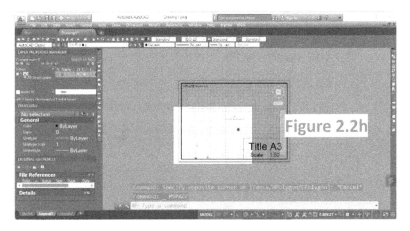

-Then press select the framework again. (I can't choose it straight now, click on all the screens and then press Shift to select Remove Paper Frame.)

-Then press the decimal number in the lower right, select Scale1:50 as shown in Figure 2.2I.

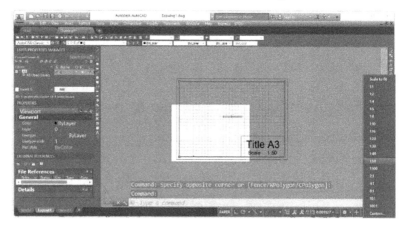

Figure 2.2I

-We will get a Scale 1:50 job as shown in Figure 2.2J. we can adjust position by double-clicking into the framework as before, but do not zoom in and out, press the PAN mouse roller only, otherwise just The scale we set will be distorted.

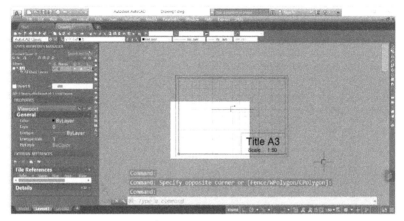

Figure 2.2J

-Then press Ctrl+P. Set as shown. 2.2k and select Window

Figure 2.2k

-Select the print region, A3 paper frame. Yes, as shown in the 2.2L picture.

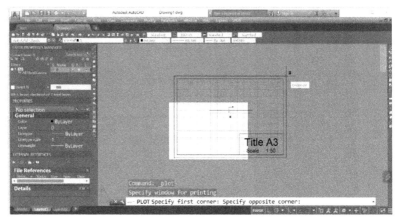

Figure 2.2L

- The actual print scale is 1mm : 1 unit because we have already set it to 1:50, so there is no need to set 1:50 when ordering Print again.

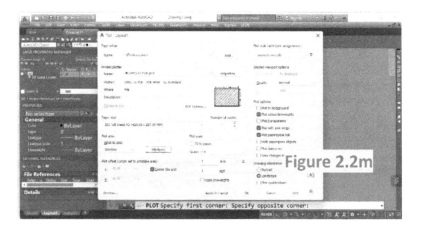

Figure 2.2m

-Press Preview to see as shown in the picture
2.2n OK and order Print!!

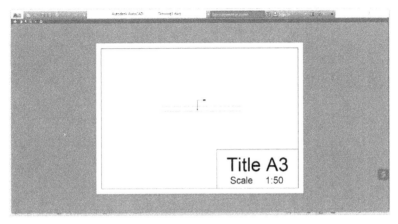

Figure 2.2n

2.3 Multi-sheet printing

-When we have many pages in the layout, we
can print at once by pressing Publish Print as
shown in picture 2.3a.

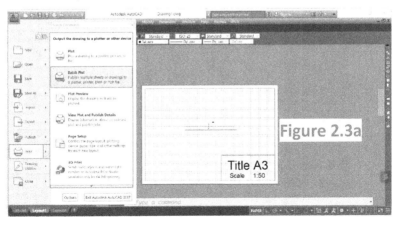

-Then let us delete selection that is not all relevant such as the Model page as shown in picture 2.3b.

Figure 2.3b

-Then click to select to the Layout page where we will print all by pressing Shift to select first and last from top to bottom will be all selections. As shown in Figure 2.3c.

-Then don't take your hand   off Shift, click on
the print settings. As shown in the picture. 2.3d
Select the name of   the Setup1 setting (we must
Save and as the value name Print before. Before
we order the normal Print first, we press add
and name Save   the Print setting. Then press it
out before you print it. Publish it)

Figure 2.3d

- Then press Browser dot 3 points as shown in
picture 2.3f, select Location to save the file after
printing.

-Then press Publish to print it. During printing, I found a question to answer NO completely. As shown in the picture 2.3g

Figure 2.3g

Chapter 3

WorkShop practicing duct drawings using basic commands

3.1 Single curved air duct

- Start us to write a pipe line first according to Figure 3.1a, we will write the pipe size 20 inches x 12 inches.

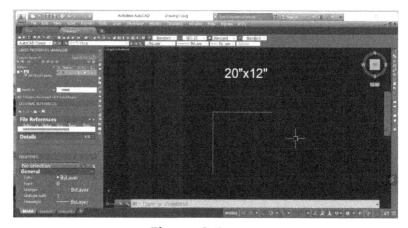

Figure 3.1a

-Then offset to 250 units or 250mm , 12 inches side. We will not be able to see it because it is the side that penetrates into the model, as shown in Figure 3.1b.

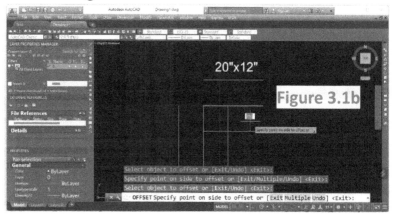

-Then use the Trim Cut command as shown in
Figure 3.1c.

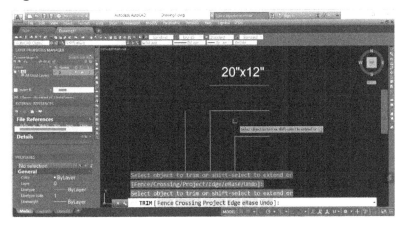

Figure 3.1c

-Then use the 100mm or 100 unit fillet
command as shown in Figure 3.1d.

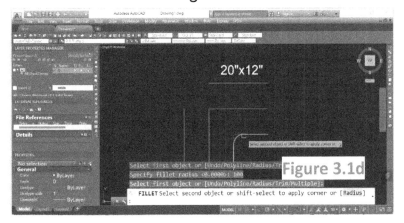

-Then offset the fillet curve to 500 units as shown in Figure 3.1e.

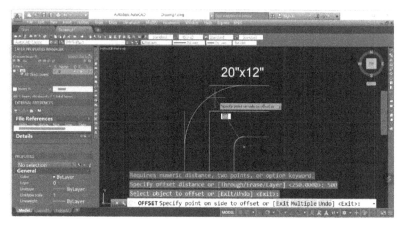

Figure 3.1e

-Then draw a line to cut the trim and finish it, it is finished as shown in the picture 3.1f.

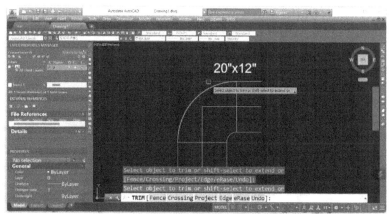

Figure 3.1f

3.2 2-way split air duct, T-shape

- Start us to write the pipe line first according to the picture 3.2a, we will write the pipe size as shown in the picture.

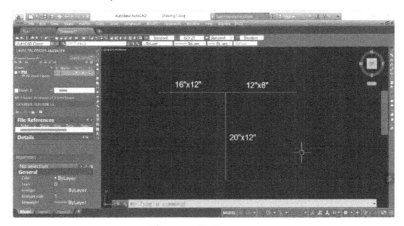

Figure 3.2a

-Then offset the pipe according to the size as shown in Figure 3.2b based mainly on the big number.

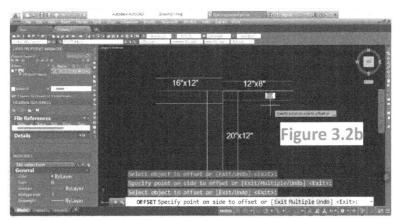

-Then using the Trim command, trim it neatly as shown. 3.2c pics

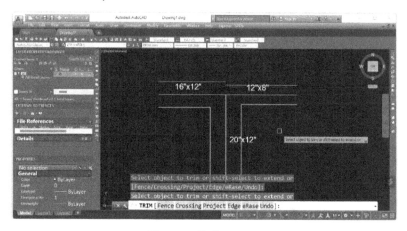

Figure 3.2c

-Then fillet as pictured. 3.2D pics, fillet distance 100mm or 100 units

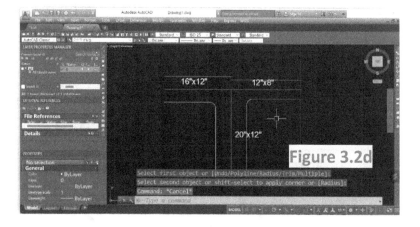

-Then, trim the line to make a large curved fillet at a distance of 350 units by calculating the distance of 100(small curved fillet distance) + 250(where the large curved fillet line is away from the pipe wall) as shown in Figure 3.2e.

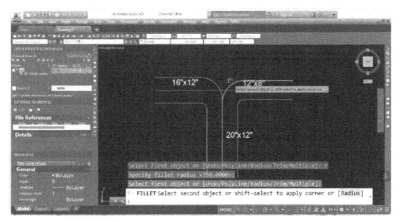

Figure 3.2e

-Then trim it neatly as shown in Figure 3.2f.

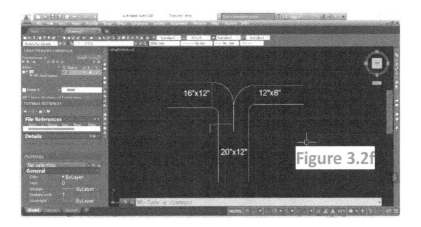

3.3 3-way separate air duct

- Start us to write the pipe line first as shown in picture 3.3a, we will write the pipe size as shown in the picture.

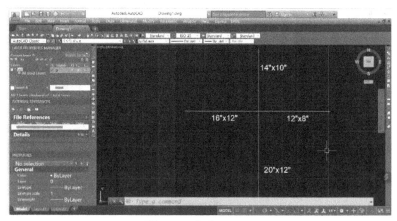

Figure 3.3a

-Then offset the pipe according to the size as shown in Figure 3.3b based mainly on the big number.

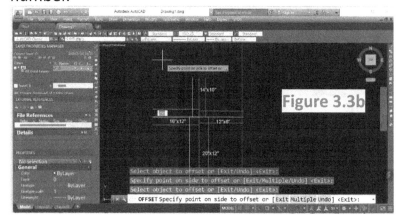

-Then using the Trim command, trim it neatly as shown. 3.3c pics

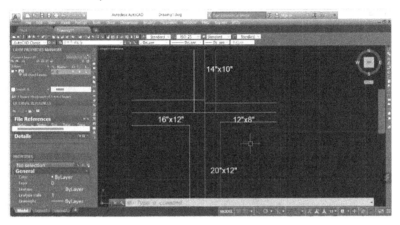

Figure 3.3c

-Then fillet as pictured. 3.3d Yes, fillet distance 100mm or 100 units.

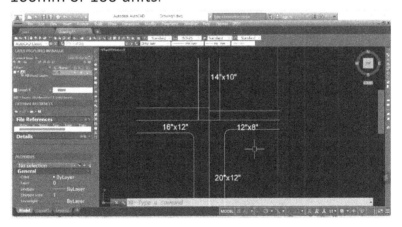

Figure 3.3d

-Then draw a line dividing the main pipe into half of the half, as shown in Figure 3.3e.

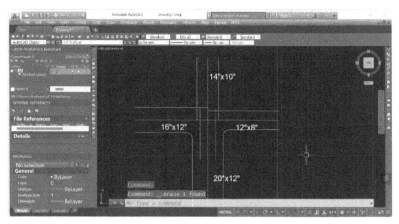

Figure 3.3e

-Trim the line   successfully, the fillet is curved big. The calculation method is the same. 100+125=225mm as pictured 3.3f

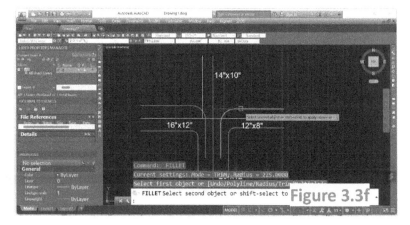

Figure 3.3f

-Trim the lines neatly according to the 3.3g
picture .

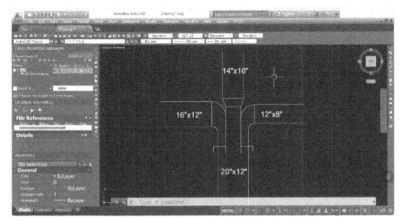

Figure 3.3g

3.4 Two way split air duct Y-shape

- Start us to write the pipe line first according to
picture 3.4a, we will write the pipe size as
shown in the picture.

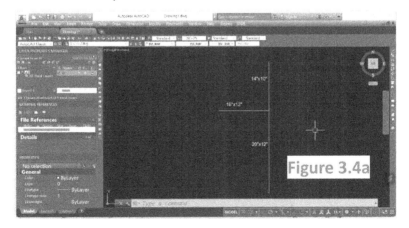

Figure 3.4a

-Then offset the pipe according to the size as shown in Figure 3.4b based mainly on the big number. It will be noticed that we will trim the move so that the split pipe wall that goes upwards to the right side   is in line with the main pipe wall on the right.

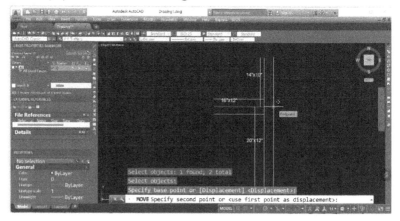

Figure 3.4b

-afterwards Using the Trim command, trim it neatly as shown. 3.4c pics

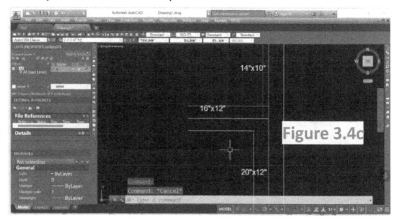

-Then fillet as pictured. 3.4D pics, fillet distance 100mm or 100 units

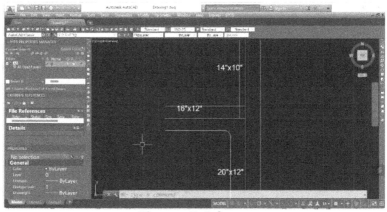

Figure 3.4d

-Trim the line successfully, the fillet curve is big (use the line that divides the main pipe in half, is the center line of the main pipe). The calculation method is the same.
100+250=350mm as shown in 3.4e picture

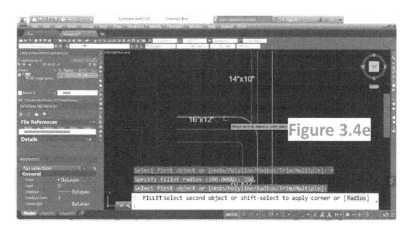

-Trim the extension tube as shown in the 3.4f
picture.

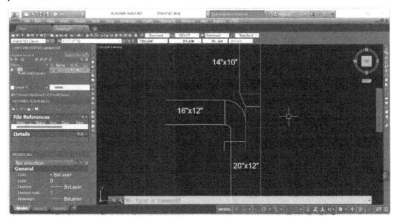

Figure 3.4f

3.5 Flex Writing

-Start by writing the end of the pipe separately
as shown in the picture 3.5a will be a symbol for
folding the pipe before inserting the flex tube.

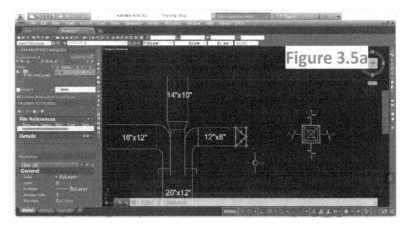

-Then, using the Polyline command, draw a line from the end of the pipe to the diffuser that we have created. In the meantime, you may use the ARC command at the end before dragging it to hit the diffuser, as shown in Figure 3.5b.

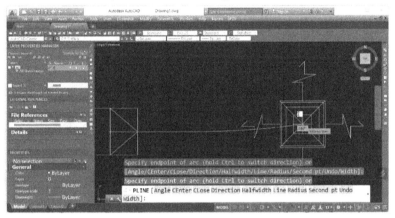

Figure 3.5b

-Then create a block. Reference Block as shown in the picture, the width is 300 units according to the pipe size and the length is about 30 units as shown in the picture 3.5c.

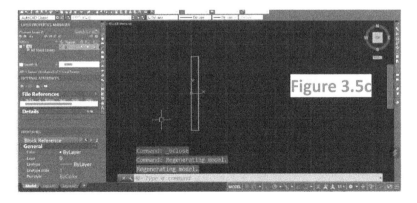

-Then run Block by Type ME enter Click the
→line Polyline Type b enter Type → the Block
→name that we set enter Type Y enter   Type a
space of about →70 →enter   is finished. 3.5d
pics

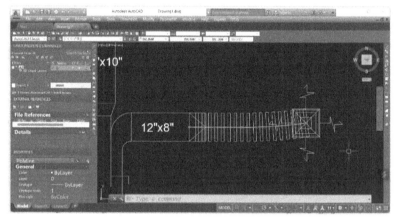

Figure 3.5d

Chapter 4

CREATING AN ON-OFF LAYER

-We can create layers of different objects that we write in autocad. As shown in Figure 4.1a, click on New Layer.

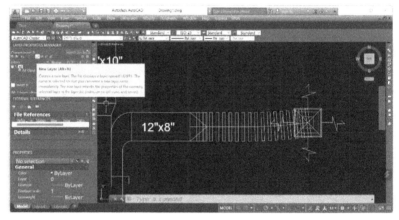

Figure 4a

-Then type the name of the layer as needed, as in the picture is the layer of the diffuser, then type the name SAG as shown in picture 4b.

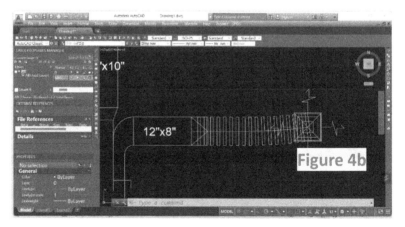

-Then click on Diffuser and select Layer as SAG
As we have created as shown in the 4c image, it
will be noticed that the diffuser color will also
follow the layer that we have created.

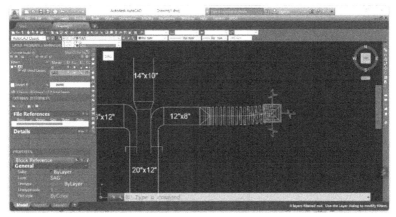

Figure 4c

-The way to use it is when we don't want to
show it. You can press off the light bulb on the
layer that we create as shown in the 4d picture.

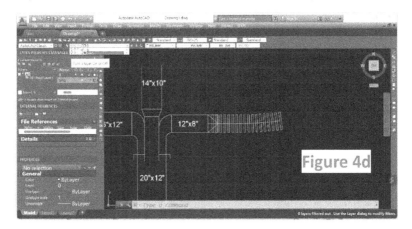

Chapter 5

Plot style Settings

and pen number colors.

-Before printing We can set the weight, the lines of the color that we print. Click as shown in the picture 5a exactly. Side photo monochrome

Figure 5a

-Since it is monochrome, the color of all the colors printed will be black as shown in picture 5b.

-However, we can adjust the line weight by
going to Line weight as shown in the picture 5c,
adjust the gray size 9 to 0.00 because it is the
color used to make the background plan, usually
the lightest. Most of the light colors are grey 8,9
and yellow Color 2 with Red Color 1, yellow and
red may be adjusted to Line weight more than
0.00 , such as 0.05, while dark colors such as
green and purple, blue, blue may be adjusted to
0.25 depending on the plot style of each
company. Red, yellow, often used with arrows,
we may use screening to help adjust the weight
of the color again, 100 is the darkest, and below
100 is faded.

Figure 5c

-When you're done adjusting. Press Save as to name Plot Style, then press Save , then Save&Close as shown in the 5D picture.

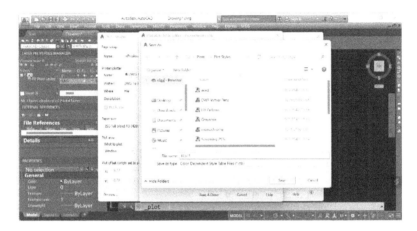

Figure 5d

THE END

www.ingramcontent.com/pod-product-compliance
Lightning Source LLC
LaVergne TN
LVHW051709050326
832903LV00032B/4102